C000093975

Original Title: FORMULA 1 - 101 RIDDLES

© FORMULA 1 - 101 RIDDLES, Carlos Martínez
Cerdá and Víctor Martínez Cerdá, 2023

Authors: Víctor Martínez Cerdá and Carlos
Martínez Cerdá (V&C Brothers)

© Cover and illustrations: V&C Brothers

Layout and design: V&C Brothers

All rights reserved. This publication may not be
reproduced, stored, recorded, or transmitted in
any form or by any means, whether mechanical,
photochemical, electronic, magnetic, electro-
optical, or through photocopies or information
retrieval systems, or any other present or future
method, without the prior written permission of
the copyright holders.

FORMULA 1
101
RIDDLES

 ALL THE ANSWERS CAN BE FOUND IN THE LAST PAGES OF THE BOOK.

1

Between speed and asphalt, there is a man of great skill who has left his mark in history and elevated his name to greatness.

He is a legendary race car driver who has won 7 championships.

His name is known worldwide, and his achievements are worthy of tales.

From his youth, he demonstrated his ability and quickly became a prodigy.

His technique and cunning have distinguished him, and he soon became a prestigious driver.

His skill was impressive, his speed astonishing, and his passion for racing, burning.

His story also had its tragedies when an accident left him injured; however, his indomitable spirit led him to fight to get back on track.

Which driver are we referring to?

a] Ayrton Senna.
b] Lewis Hamilton.
c] Michael Schumacher.

2

In an enchanted forest, among the mountains, there is a track full of curves and valleys.

The engines roar, and the crowds get excited with each lap, as the drivers surpass themselves.

Time is treacherous in this place; rain appears without warning, making the challenge even more dangerous and testing the driver's skill in the cold.

It is a challenge in itself where the hearts of 70,000 spectators race as they watch the cars go by and the tires screech on the turns, holding their breath.

In this magical place, many stories have been written to be remembered, like great championships and thrilling races, and moments of glory that will forever remain in the minds of enthusiasts.

Which circuit are we referring to?

a) Monza.
b) Silverstone.
c) Spa-Francorchamps.

3

In the world of motorsport, there is a legend about a renowned and traditional racing team that has been the most beloved and feared for years, leaving its mark on the track.

It was born in Maranello, Italy, in the 1940s, founded by the "Comendatore," whose passion for speed and desire for victory were his true driving force.

With its famous prancing horse logo and unmistakable red color, it has left an indelible mark in Formula 1 and throughout the visible world.

Throughout its history, it has had many drivers, great names who have made their mark, such as Juan Manuel Fangio, Niki Lauda, and Michael Schumacher, who have raised the flag of this team to the top.

It has also had great engineers like Mauro Forghieri and John Barnard, who have created machines that have made history with their design, technology, and speed.

However, it hasn't been all victory and glory, as it has also experienced defeats and failures, but it has always known how to rise and move forward.

Today, it remains an important team with a large budget and many resources, and despite having difficult and challenging seasons, it always rises and moves forward with strength and courage.

Which racing team are we referring to?

a) Ferrari.
b) Williams.
c) Lotus.

4

On the track where engines roar and the atmosphere is pure excitement, there have been many renowned drivers who have left their mark in the history of this competition.

Among them is the driver whose name became news in 1982 at the San Marino Grand Prix when he won the race in a car that seemed perfect but was soon discovered to have incorrect weight.

The FIA disqualified the driver in question because the car was underweight, a violation of the rules governing the competition, and the driver lost his victory, causing great disappointment.

This character has achieved 23 victories and 3 world championships in his career, becoming one of the greatest drivers in the history of F1.

Who was the driver we are referring to?

a) Ayrton Senna.
b) Alain Prost.
c) Nelson Piquet.

5

Among Formula 1 drivers, there are two who stand out above the rest and have been part of one of the most intense and legendary rivalries in the history of this sport.

They first faced each other in the 2007 season when they shared a team at McLaren. From the beginning, tension was palpable, and disputes between them were constant.

The rivalry between them intensified as the season progressed, reaching its climax at the Hungarian Grand Prix when the McLaren team favored one of them in a controversial decision that harmed the other.

This incident caused a crisis within the team, and one of them left McLaren at the end of the season.

Since then, both drivers have competed for different teams, but their rivalry has endured over time.

They have been involved in epic races and duels while maintaining a tense yet respectful relationship.

Which drivers are we referring to?

a) Michael Schumacher and Mika Hakkinen.
b) Lewis Hamilton and Fernando Alonso.
c) Sebastian Vettel and Mark Webber.

6

In the world of Formula 1, not only do the drivers compete for the championship, but the teams also compete for a valuable trophy.

The best engineers work tirelessly to design the best cars, each one faster than the previous.

These teams engage in a constant race to develop advanced technology and aerodynamic components, allowing them to win races and earn crucial points for the championship standings.

The competition is fierce, and every detail matters, from adjustments in the suspension to changes in race strategy.

The teams must always be alert, ready to improve their performance on the track and win the precious trophy.

The racing teams strive to earn the necessary points by working hard to win races and reach the podium.

The trophy is the recognition of their skill and hard work, a reward for their dedication to the sport of Formula 1.

Which trophy are we referring to?

a) Formula 1 Constructors' Championship.
b) Formula 1 Teams' Trophy.
c) Formula 1 Manufacturers' Cup.

7

In a place where drivers display their bravery and skill, there was a tragic incident.

At the 1994 San Marino Grand Prix, a driver famous for his talent and courage suffered a fatal accident in the paddock.

He passed away due to a severe crash at the Tamburello corner during the race.

A suspension rod from the vehicle penetrated his helmet visor, causing a fatal head injury.

The driver in question, who had already won 2 championships and was vying for a third, became newsworthy at that moment due to his tragic fate, which caused great sorrow.

Who was that driver?

a) Lewis Hamilton.
b) Michael Schumacher.
c) Ayrton Senna.

8

I am an Italian luxury brand, and my name is synonymous with elegance and fashion.

With a past in Formula 1 that adorns me, my designs are a true display of audacity.

My logo is a portrayal of Medusa, which gives me a distinctive touch.

I sponsored Formula 1 teams with my style and elegance.

My Formula 1-inspired clothing line is a tribute to speed and innovation, with a sophisticated and avant-garde style that embodies the perfection of my brand.

Which brand are we referring to?

a) Gucci.
b) Versace.
c) Armani.

9

On the most famous racing tracks, there is a man of great talent and speed who has left his mark in history and reached the pinnacle of immortal glory.

He is an exceptional racing driver who has won 7 World Championships, and his name resonates worldwide, as his success is worthy of legendary tales.

From his childhood, he demonstrated his skill and quickly became a prodigy.

His technique and cunning set him apart, and his competitive spirit was astonishing.

He has made his mark with his incredible speed and technique, surpassing the world's best drivers, showcasing his prodigious courage and valor.

But his story has also involved struggles against racism and discrimination in sports, fighting for equality and justice, becoming a role model.

Who are we referring to?

a) Michael Schumacher.
b) Fernando Alonso.
c) Lewis Hamilton.

10

In a place of legends, there is a race circuit that is famous worldwide.

With a length of 5.891 kilometers, it is a challenging circuit with tight corners and long straights that make the driver sweat.

Inaugurated in 1948, it was one of the first of its kind and to this day remains a challenge for any daring pilot.

Great moments of joy have been experienced there, and although the competition is tough, there is a great sense of harmony in the air.

If you visit it one day, you will feel the excitement in the air, and even if you're not a driver, you will enjoy an unparalleled spectacle.

Which circuit are we referring to?

a) Monaco Circuit.
b) Silverstone Circuit.
c) Hungaroring Circuit.

11

In the world of speed, there is a racing team that shines on its own, with an engine that is a masterpiece and a history that is a true gem.

It is a team that has managed to prevail with talented and skilled drivers, and technology that always surprises.

Based in Brackley, England, and backed by the star brand, it has excelled in the fastest competition on the planet.

Since its return to the category in 2010, it has achieved great victories and championships with names like Hamilton and Rosberg, who have left their mark in the history of Formula 1.

But this team doesn't rely solely on drivers, as it also boasts an elite technical team that has created a high-powered hybrid engine and aerodynamics that always fascinate.

Today, it remains a feared team with a budget that knows no limits, and although it has faced strong and competitive rivals, it has always remained at the top of the standings.

Which team are we referring to?

a) Mercedes-AMG Petronas.
b) Aston Martin.
c) Alpine F1 Team.

12

In a place where speed is an obsession and drivers challenge each other in every competition, there was a major scandal at the Belgian Grand Prix when a driver was disqualified, and the news became public.

This world champion driver had won the race with great skill and dedication, but upon technical inspection, it was discovered that their car was not in compliance with the regulations, and the disqualification was enforced, causing great disappointment.

Nevertheless, this driver has achieved seven championships, a mythical accomplishment, and although their career has been impeccable, this incident will be remembered as a disqualification in a great race that caused great uproar.

However, this character did not let this setback defeat them and continued to fight with great determination and faith, showcasing their talent and bravery in every race.

Today, they still stand as a great legend and a shining star.

Which driver are we referring to?

a) Fernando Alonso.
b) Sebastian Vettel.
c) Lewis Hamilton.

13

The roar of engines and speed on the track are the elements of a well-known rivalry between two renowned racing titans.

During the 80s and 90s, the golden era of Formula 1, these two giants dominated with their talents and strategies, although they had their differences.

In 1988, both coincided as teammates and rivals at McLaren.

Both wanted to win, to be the best of the season, and that's how an relentless battle began, without camaraderie.

In Japan in 1989, both collided in a risky corner.

One of them won the race, but controversy ensued.

In 1990, the story repeated itself in Suzuka, but the other emerged victorious, while excitement, euphoria, and jubilation erupted.

Three years together at McLaren, and their legacy is marked.

A legendary rivalry that is still remembered, between two greats of the track who made history and continue to be an example of passion and glory.

Which drivers are we referring to?

a) Nigel Mansell and Nelson Piquet.
b) Ayrton Senna and Alain Prost.
c) Riccardo Patrese and Thierry Boutsen.

14

In Formula 1, excitement is constant, and drivers strive to win every moment.

But sometimes, the race doesn't start well, and drivers must make a furious comeback from the back.

At the 2008 Italian Grand Prix, a driver surprised the world with their remarkable feat.

Starting from 15th position, they managed to claim victory, delivering a dream-like race.

It was a race full of emotions and drama, with spectacular overtakes that ignited great excitement.

Although many thought the race was decided, this driver didn't give up and achieved the least expected victory.

Who was that driver who accomplished this unparalleled feat?

a) Lewis Hamilton.
b) Fernando Alonso.
c) Sebastian Vettel.

15

I am a highly coveted award, the dream of every racer whose performance has been outstanding, earning praise from fans and experts alike.

My design is a work of art with smooth curves and a solid base, crafted with the finest materials and attention to the smallest detail.

I am presented at the end of each season in a ceremony that brings together the best of Formula 1, where the winner receives a thunderous applause.

Who am I?

a) The Formula 1 World Championship Trophy.
b) The Laureus World Sports Award for Athlete of the Year.
c) The Princess of Asturias Award for Sports.

16

In Mediterranean lands, you will find me at a historic circuit where up to 118,000 voices roar with excitement, an opportunity you should not miss, as speed and fascination are what you will find here, with a long straight and curves that should not be underestimated.

I am an iconic race in the Formula 1 calendar, where drivers relentlessly battle for victory.

My name is a country and a passion that come alive in every fan.

Who am I?

a) The Italian Grand Prix at Monza.
b) The San Marino Grand Prix at Imola.
c) The European Grand Prix in Valencia.

17

I am a prestigious brand.

My passion is speed and precision.

My emblem of three diamonds is a great challenge, and sponsoring F1 is my greatest ambition.

I am recognized for my engineering and focus on innovation, with a style and elegance that captivates and a presence that catches the eye.

My brand is present in F1, with a dedicated and passionate team.

Our engines are a true engineering masterpiece, and our commitment has always been outstanding.

If speed is your passion and precision is your obsession, you should consider my brand for ultimate satisfaction.

Which brand are we referring to?

a) Lamborghini.
b) Porsche.
c) Mitsubishi.

18

On the Formula 1 tracks, a German driver showcases his skill and passion with 4 world championships under his belt, as he is one of the greats of the competition.

With his ability and great intelligence, he has mastered the races with finesse.

This driver is a true strategy genius.

He has piloted for renowned teams like Red Bull and Ferrari, and his speed and focus have led him to conquer glory.

With his aggressive and daring driving style, he has left a mark in the history of the sport, and although he has had ups and downs in his career, he has never lost his love for competition.

He is a driver who always seeks perfection and never gives up in the face of adversity.

His competitive spirit and great dedication have led him to achieve excellence.

Who are we referring to?

a) Michael Schumacher.
b) Lewis Hamilton.
c) Sebastian Vettel.

19

Between the sea and the mountains lies a jewel of Formula 1.

It is a track as narrow as it is elegant, which makes the drivers sweat with excitement.

With its famous corner at the casino and the finish straight at the harbor, it is a legendary circuit that no driver forgets.

From Graham Hill to Ayrton Senna, passing through Fangio and Schumacher, all have left their mark in this place where skill and bravery come together.

Every year, the race is a spectacle that attracts fans from around the world, and although its streets are not the widest, this circuit always reigns as the king of asphalt.

Which circuit are we referring to?

a) Circuit of the Americas.
b) Circuit Gilles Villeneuve.
c) Circuit de Monaco.

20

In Formula 1, there is a team whose name is synonymous with engineering.

Based in Woking, England, their races are a tribute to skill.

Founded in 1963 by Bruce, initially he was the main driver, but over time the company grew, and today it is one of the most famous and beloved.

Among their most notable achievements are 8 constructor championships won.

They have also achieved 12 driver championships, thanks to great names like Senna, Prost, and Button.

With Mercedes-Benz engines and sponsorships from major brands like Gulf and Castrol, they are an elite team that never ceases to amaze with their dynamism and speed.

Which team are we referring to?

a) Ferrari.
b) Red Bull Racing.
c) McLaren.

21

In Formula 1, there are drivers who stand out for their talent and skill as they dominate the track.

In 2005, there was one particular driver who became the youngest world champion in history.

In Renault, he found a fabulous team with which he won 2 consecutive championships in 2005 and 2006.

At just 24 years old, he made history by becoming the youngest champion, showcasing his prowess and great ability.

Who is the driver I am referring to?

a) Lewis Hamilton.
b) Sebastian Vettel.
c) Fernando Alonso.

22

In the world of racing, with fast and powerful cars, a driver stood out for his cunning and intelligence.

In the 1983 Brazilian Grand Prix, this driver achieved victory, but he couldn't savor it.

The reason was that it was discovered that his car had illegal fuel, and as a result, he was disqualified.

This Brazilian driver, with 3 championships to his name, was a legend of Formula 1, and his name is still remembered with pleasure.

Who are we referring to?

a] Nelson Piquet.
b] Alain Prost.
c] Ayrton Senna.

23

From the asphalt, the roar of engines that aspire to glory can be heard.

On the track, rivalry is a challenge between two highly experienced drivers.

Both compete in an unparalleled competition, as each one pursues victory regardless of what may happen.

In their track record, they have great feats like significant wins and podium finishes, and on the track, there is no respite or cunning, only the determination to be the best driver.

They are united by their passion for Formula 1 and adrenaline, but also by the healthy competition that makes their rivalry divine.

One is from the highlands and the other from where kangaroos live.

a) Rubens Barrichello and Jacques Villeneuve.
b) Juan Pablo Montoya and Kimi Räikkönen.
c) David Coulthard and Mark Webber.

24

With bright colors and elegant details, I rest on the head of the fastest of drivers, who has made history in the most thrilling races and left their mark on the circuits.

I am the symbol of youthful talent, the prize that indicates who is the most skillful behind the wheel and who dominates with mastery and skill.

My shape is modern and covers the champion's head with logos and emblems that denote the brand of a sport that is pure passion.

My colors change according to the team, and my design varies each season, but I am always the object of desire for those who seek to achieve glory on the tracks.

I am the symbol of success in racing, the trophy that every aspiring young driver dreams of, aiming to be the best in the most challenging tests.

Who am I?

a) The cap of the youngest driver to set a fastest lap in qualifying.
b) The flag of the team of the youngest driver to set a fastest lap in qualifying.
c) The helmet of the youngest driver to set a fastest lap in qualifying.

25

In the land of green meadows, a race is celebrated where the track becomes a challenge with curves and elevation changes that provoke excitement and cheers.

It is the most famous circuit in the region, a place that drivers must master to win with passion.

This race has been held since 1950 on a circuit of over 7 kilometers, which is a true test for the cunning driver, known for its iconic Eau Rouge corner, which drivers take at high speed and requires courage and skill to overcome its complexity.

The landscape of the Ardennes surrounds the circuit with its natural beauty, a place that becomes vibrant and full of adrenaline when the competition begins, where drivers fight for victory and the podium in an exciting race where everyone seeks to stand out and show their impressive talent.

What do you think is the correct answer?

a) German Grand Prix.
b) European Grand Prix.
c) Belgian Grand Prix.

26

On the race track, you will find me with my highly efficient and fast tires.

My wheel logo is a symbol of excellence, and I sponsor with great expertise in Formula 1.

My compounds are designed to last and withstand the high temperatures of the track.

In tight corners and endless straights, my tires keep you in competition.

My Italian brand is recognized worldwide for its quality, performance, and prestige, and in Formula 1, I am a constant presence.

Who am I?

a) Bridgestone.
b) Pirelli.
c) Goodyear.

27

His name is like an anthem in motorsport, a Brazilian driver who was unparalleled.

Winner of races and unmatched championships, his style on the track was very special.

He was born in Sao Paulo in 1956, and by the age of twenty-two, he was already the king.

With a black and yellow car from John Player Special, this driver won brilliantly at Watkins Glen.

After leaving Lotus, he joined McLaren, where he achieved his second title without faltering.

In the 1974 season, this character crowned himself again effortlessly.

But not everything was glory in his career, as in the following years, the results were not as good, and he decided to seek new directions.

Eventually, he moved to the CART category with great results.

Who are we referring to?

a) Nelson Piquet.
b) Emerson Fittipaldi.
c) Juan Pablo Montoya.

28

In a distant land where cherry trees blossom, there is a magical circuit where engines roar with power.

It is a place of emotions, speed, and adrenaline, where the bravest pilots come to compete with skill.

Its design is astonishing, a mix of tight curves, long straights, and fast corners.

The sound of engines resonates in every corner, and the atmosphere is so electric that even the clouds stir.

There, the most daring pilots push their skills to the limit in every turn, accelerating without fear.

While the crowd cheers and the mechanics work, the pilots fight for victory without taking a break.

Great battles and moments of glory have taken place in this location, where up to 155,000 souls cheer.

The greatest have triumphed there, leaving their mark in history.

It is a magical place filled with passion and excitement, and even after the race ends, it will always remain in our hearts.

Which circuit are we referring to?

a) Istanbul Circuit.
b) Hungaroring Circuit.
c) Suzuka Circuit.

29

There is a team that always amazes the audience with its speed.

Based in Milton Keynes, England, their legacy is legendary.

It was founded in 2004 by Dietrich Mateschitz with the intention of creating a team that would make an impact, and they certainly achieved it—winning their first Grand Prix in Monaco in just 2 years.

The Austrian Christian Horner is their team principal, and Max Verstappen and Sergio Pérez are their esteemed drivers.

It is a team that is not afraid to take risks, and their innovative strategies are always devised to win.

With Honda engines currently powering them and sponsorships from big brands like Aston Martin and Puma, they are an unstoppable force that never ceases to challenge the limits of speed.

Among these three teams, tell me which one is correct:

a) Mercedes-AMG Petronas F1 Team.
b) Alpine F1 Team.
c) Red Bull Racing.

30

On a May day at the urban circuit of Monte Carlo, the engine echoes.

Among narrow and dangerous curves, the pilots face a challenge.

One of them, skillful and cunning, drove his single-seater without fear.

He fought with strength, and in the end, victory was his honor.

The excitement was palpable in the air, and the stands were filled with fans.

The pilot remained in the lead while his rivals fell behind.

But on the last lap, something strange happened: the fuel ran out without warning.

With his heart in his mouth and nerves on edge, the pilot remained calm and continued on the track.

His competitors were dangerously approaching, seizing the opportunity.

But the pilot didn't give up and, with a final effort, crossed the finish line.

Amid applause and celebration, his great feat became evident.

A Monaco Grand Prix won despite the lack of fuel in his machinery.

Which pilot was able to accomplish such a feat?

a) Riccardo Patrese.
b) Ayrton Senna.
c) Alain Prost.

31

At the Imola circuit, during the 1994 San Marino Grand Prix, a very singular event occurred, which went down in Formula 1 history as one of the most controversial episodes.

In this race, a driver finished in second place after his team engaged in unethical behavior at the finish line.

This Brazilian-born driver began his Formula 1 career in 1993 and throughout his trajectory achieved 11 victories, 68 podium finishes, and 14 pole positions.

His talent on the track led him to compete for different teams like Ferrari, Brawn GP, and Williams.

But in the 1994 San Marino Grand Prix, this individual failed to cross the finish line in second place under his own power.

During the final lap of the race, his car ran out of fuel and lost speed.

However, when he reached the finish line, his team pushed him to cross in second place, triggering a great controversy.

Who are we referring to?

a) Rubens Barrichello.
b) Michael Schumacher.
c) Ayrton Senna.

32

In the Formula 1 track, rivalry is common, and often teammates also face off in a battle for the championship.

Such is the case of two teammates at Mercedes who have experienced many moments of tension and competitiveness on the track, fighting for team leadership and race supremacy.

One of them, a six-time world champion, has been the undisputed leader of the Mercedes team since his arrival in 2013.

His aggressive and precise driving style has taken him to the top of the sport, accumulating numerous victories and records.

The other is a Finnish driver who joined Mercedes in 2017 and has been a solid and loyal competitor within the team.

However, he has often struggled to keep up with his teammate's pace and has had to settle for second place on several occasions.

The rivalry between the two has intensified in recent seasons as they compete for the Formula 1 World Championship title.

In the 2019 season, the first driver won the championship, but the other was not far behind, finishing in second place in the overall standings.

In the 2020 season, they faced each other on the track once again, and although one driver claimed the championship for the seventh time, the other proved to be a formidable competitor, finishing in second place in the standings.

However, despite the on-track rivalry, both have shown to be good teammates off the track.

Who are we talking about?

a) Lewis Hamilton and Valtteri Bottas.
b) Michael Schumacher and Nico Rosberg.
c) Sebastian Vettel and Mark Webber.

33

I am the desire of every racing driver, the goal of speed and skill, the prize awarded to those who overcome barriers and demonstrate their prowess on every track and in every city.

My form is that of a highly attractive object, with elegant and sophisticated details, a trophy that symbolizes competitiveness and rewards those who achieve the best results.

During the racing season, I am sought after, every driver wants to be my owner, for they know that winning me is what brings triumph and showcases their talent with determination.

To claim me, more than victories are needed, as it requires speed and determination and a burning desire to surpass the stories of those who have dominated the competition.

My colors vary depending on the event, and my design changes each season, but I am always the most coveted prize sought by the most ambitious and dedicated pilot.

I am the reward for effort and passion, the plaque that honors the best driver, the award that symbolizes excitement.

Who am I?

a) The trophy for the fastest driver of the season.
b) The DHL Fastest Lap Award.
c) The medal for the driver with the most fastest laps in the season.

34

In the eastern land, a grand prix is celebrated on a unique circuit within an amusement park.

Its linked curves and changes in elevation make the pilots showcase their skill and concentration.

Its history is very ancient, as it is a continuous race on the Formula 1 calendar.

Fans flock to every corner of the circuit to see the pilots challenge the asphalt and time.

The trees of the forest surround the track, and people cheer wildly because the challenge is great, but the reward is greater for those who cross the finish line in first place.

Which race are we referring to?

a) Chinese Grand Prix.
b) Singapore Grand Prix.
c) Japanese Grand Prix.

35

In the world of motorsport, I make my presence known, as my brand is synonymous with excellent lubrication.

I sponsor in F1 with great quality and efficiency, my logo is a gorilla, a symbol of strength and consistency.

My products are famous for their endurance and reliability, they are used by many in the world of high speed.

My oils and lubricants are synonymous with excellence, and in F1, my presence is a true testament.

Who am I?

a) Motul.
b) Castrol.
c) Shell Helix.

36

In the Formula 1 circuits, there is a driver who brings excitement with his bravery and great passion, as he has earned the respect of the entire fanbase.

With 2 world titles under his belt, he is one of the greatest in history, as his skill and great prowess make him a true glory.

His career has been a roller coaster, with great victories and also setbacks, but he has always shown his fighting and courageous spirit.

He has driven for renowned teams such as Renault, Ferrari, and McLaren, and his skill behind the wheel is such that he has been called the "King of Overtaking."

He is an intelligent and strategic driver who knows how to take advantage of any situation, and although luck is not always on his side, he is always willing to give his best performance.

His determination and passion for racing have won the hearts of many fans, and his competitive spirit is an inspiration for those who pursue their dreams with tenacity.

Who is the driver in this riddle?

a) Michael Schumacher.
b) Lewis Hamilton.
c) Fernando Alonso.

37

Known for its twisting layout filled with fast and slow corners, it is a circuit beloved by Formula 1 enthusiasts.

With its famous Senna S on the straight and its Lago corner, it is a challenge for any racing driver.

Since its inauguration in the 1970s, it has witnessed great races and emotions.

The relentless battle among the drivers for victory makes the audience thrill with each of their actions.

Located in São Paulo, Brazil, it has a rich history and charisma.

Its up to 60,000 passionate fans fill every grandstand, regardless of the sun and rain, as nothing can stop them.

Which circuit are we referring to?

a) Interlagos.
b) Silverstone Circuit.
c) Spa-Francorchamps Circuit.

38

In Formula 1, there is a team with a rich history and a great track record. Based in Enstone, their legacy is eternal.

It was founded in 1977 under the name Toleman and changed ownership over time until becoming Renault.

The team has had great drivers like Frenchman Alain Prost, who won 2 championships.

The Spanish Fernando Alonso is their main driver, and he is accompanied by the Frenchman Esteban Ocon.

It is a team that is not afraid to innovate, and its commitment to the environment is its unique hallmark.

With Renault engines and sponsorships from major brands like Groupama and MAPFRE, it is a fast force.

With 2 constructor championships and 3 driver championships in their record, they always stand out for their efficiency and skill.

Which team are we referring to?

a) AlphaTauri.
b) Alpine F1 Team.
c) Williams Racing.

39

In the 1980s in Formula 1, a driver switched teams with great excitement, hoping to showcase his skills and win races.

It was in the 1986 season when this character took a big risk, leaving his previous team and joining the powerful McLaren team.

The season started a bit slow, but he quickly adapted to his new machine, and in the second half of the season, he began to reap victories with great satisfaction.

It was an intense battle with his teammate, who was also fast and very cunning, but our driver remained focused, and in the final race, the title was secured.

Which driver are we referring to?

a) Ayrton Senna.
b) Nelson Piquet.
c) Alain Prost.

40

In the last lap of the 2002 Austrian Grand Prix, something unprecedented happened in Formula 1.

The two drivers from the Ferrari team were leading the race and heading towards a double victory for the team.

However, in the final corner, one of them ordered the other to let his car pass and win the race in an attempt to help their team score points for the World Drivers' Championship.

Reluctantly, the driver obeyed and allowed his teammate to overtake him and win the race.

Fans and the press criticized Ferrari's maneuver, arguing that it was unsportsmanlike and undermined the integrity of the sport.

As a result, new rules were introduced in Formula 1 to prevent teams from favoring one driver over another.

Which drivers are we referring to?

a) Michael Schumacher and Rubens Barrichello.
b) Juan Pablo Montoya and David Coulthard.
c) Niki Lauda and Alberto Ascari.

41

On the scorching asphalt of the track, two warriors face each other with skill, fighting for the title and glory in a rivalry that knows no truce or rest.

One of them, cunning and fast, a four-time world champion with an aggressive and determined style, has reached the top of the podium.

The other, a master of technique, with the skill of a virtuoso behind the wheel, has captivated fans with his precise and elegant driving.

On multiple occasions, they have collided, each determined to surpass the other, in a battle that has been epic and kept the audience on the edge of their seats.

The whole world has witnessed their thrilling and fierce duels that have left an indelible mark in the history of Formula 1.

Which drivers are we referring to?

a) Sebastian Vettel and Fernando Alonso.
b) Lewis Hamilton and Fernando Alonso.
c) Michael Schumacher and Fernando Alonso.

42

I am the most desired object in competition, the symbol of victory and glory, as well as the reward for effort and dedication, and the goal of every driver who aspires to be immortalized in history.

My shape is that of a thrilling trophy with elegant and sophisticated details.

In 2022, I was made of wood and water.

I always symbolize talent and reward those who overcome the most challenging obstacles.

My home is the longest track of the season, a legendary and thrilling circuit where skill and ability are necessary to reach the finish line and admiration.

My colors vary according to the edition, and my design changes every year, but I am always the most exciting prize sought by the most determined and ambitious driver.

Since my origin, many champions have raised my cup with great emotion, leaving their mark on the competitions and the history of this passionate sport.

What trophy am I referring to?

a) Trophy of the Spanish Grand Prix.
b) Trophy of the Belgian Grand Prix.
c) Trophy of the Monaco Grand Prix.

43

In a corner of the world where samba and vibrant colors reign, a race is celebrated where the engines never stop roaring.

An demanding and thrilling circuit that tests the endless skill of the drivers.

With a very long straight and a tight corner, the drivers showcase their unfailing expertise.

In Formula 1, it is a renowned race, as fans eagerly await the event to see their favorite drivers on the pavement.

Which prize are we referring to?

a) Mexican Grand Prix.
b) Brazilian Grand Prix.
c) Canadian Grand Prix.

44

Amidst the roar of engines and the frenzy of competition, my brand stands tall with strength and determination.

If technology excites you and cutting-edge is your passion, you cannot miss seeing my name and sponsorship.

In Formula 1, my presence is synonymous with innovation, and my tree logo symbolizes my commitment to ecology and sustainability, as I seek not only success on the track but also the preservation of nature and society.

I am a globally renowned brand of fuels and lubricants with a history and legacy that make me stand out.

My unmistakable red and yellow colors shine in the competition, and my name is a word that resonates with strength and passion.

Which brand are we referring to?

a) BP.
b) ExxonMobil.
c) Shell.

45

Among curves and straightaways, swift as the wind,
a young driver with great talent emerged.

Surely you must know him, a prodigious boy has become.

Born in the Netherlands, in a racing household, his father
was a driver who left good traces.

At the age of 4, he was already handling a kart, and since then,
he hasn't stopped piloting.

At just 18 years old, he made himself known, entered Formula
1 to prove himself, and despite his youth and little experience,
he left the audience speechless.

On the track, he is a true predator, with his skills, there is
no one who can match him in his work.

He is agile, intelligent, brave, fast, and has the fierceness
of a true predator.

He has conquered podiums and achieved victories, and he
doesn't stop, as he strives for more in his trajectory.

Which driver are we referring to?

a) Lionel Messi.
b) Cristiano Ronaldo.
c) Max Verstappen.

46

Over in the Ardennes in the region of Wallonia, there is a legendary circuit in F1 that is a gem.

With its legendary curves, incredible ups and downs, it is a challenge for drivers as there is no time for distractions.

The 7 kilometers of the track are a great challenge as the drivers must be ready for the pace and the cold.

The weather is always uncertain due to rain and fog, but it makes the race more enticing.

Memorable moments have been experienced on this circuit with Senna, Schumacher, and Hamilton, all of them are unforgettable.

The Eau Rouge and Blanchimont curves are the most feared, as only the bravest can come out unscathed.

And while it is a historic circuit, it should also be noted that sometimes the race becomes a bit boring to watch, but with the changes and surprises that sometimes arise, it never fails to entertain.

Which circuit are we referring to?

a) Spa-Francorchamps.
b) Circuit Paul Ricard.
c) Circuit of the Americas (COTA).

47

In the F1 Grand Circus, the race is a feat, as the drivers must fight with all their strength and skill.

Speed and curves are the most lethal tests, and the high temperatures cause the drivers to weaken.

That's why it's common to hear that drivers lose weight, perhaps even kilos, in each race.

There are 20 competitors fighting in each Grand Prix, and if they complete the laps, it's likely that they will lose weight.

The reason for this suffering is the narrow cockpit where the temperature rises, and the G-forces are a challenge.

But despite this, the drivers continue because F1 is a passion that fuels the heart.

Approximately how much weight do the drivers lose in a race?

a) Up to 4 kg of weight.
b) Up to 6 kg of weight.
c) Up to 2 kg of weight.

48

Among the many numbers that can adorn Formula 1 cars, there is one that has become a rarity.

The number 13, which is considered unlucky in many countries, has been very rarely used throughout the history of this sport.

Only on 2 occasions has a car with the number 13 been seen on the starting grid of an F1 Grand Prix.

The first time was in the 1963 Mexican Grand Prix when a driver decided to use it; however, his luck was not particularly good as he had an accident in the first lap and couldn't complete the race.

The second time the number 13 appeared in Formula 1 was in the 1976 British Grand Prix.

On this occasion, another driver carried it on his car.

This character didn't have much better luck than the previous one, as he failed to qualify for the race and was left out of the grid.

And although superstition shouldn't have a place in sports, it seems that in this case, the drivers prefer to avoid that number.

Which drivers used the number 13?

a) Moisés Solana and Divina Galica.
b) Jim Clark and Jackie Stewart.
c) Ayrton Senna and Alain Prost.

49

Between two Formula 1 drivers, a rivalry emerged.

In 2009, an epic race took place in Malaysia.

One of them achieved the podium and celebrated, but the other wasn't far behind, and throughout the season, their competitiveness showed.

In the 2012 Brazilian Grand Prix, destiny brought them together, and both drivers engaged in an impressive battle.

One secured the pole position, but the other fought until the end, and despite setbacks, their determination was crucial.

In the 2013 Monaco Grand Prix, one of them claimed victory, but the competition was intense.

The other chased them all the way, and although they didn't win, they demonstrated their talent with passion and dedication.

Therefore, the rivalry between them was undoubtedly a memorable confrontation, and although it may not compare to others, its intensity is admirable.

The possible answers for other drivers could be:

a) Lewis Hamilton and Sebastian Vettel.
b) Max Verstappen and Charles Leclerc.
c) Nico Rosberg and Jenson Button.

50

From my throne, I observe the circuit with sharp curves and long straights.

The drivers are eager, prepared, and ready in search of the glory that my form holds.

I am the coveted prize of each season, the object that every driver longs to win, as it entails the work and dedication of completing the highest number of laps without stopping.

My shape is impressive with precise details.

I am a shining plate of splendor and brilliance, a symbol of excellence and effort, bestowed upon the victor with great honor.

Every lap is a battle, an endless struggle against time, against the circuit, against rivals, and the driver who manages to conquer them all becomes deserving of my special trophy.

Which prize am I referring to?

a) The Trophy for the Driver with the Most Completed Laps.
b) The Award for the Most Resilient Driver of the Season.
c) The Distinction for the Most Persevering Driver in the Competition.

51

In a city in East Asia, an urban circuit has been built where drivers showcase their skills in a nighttime and entertaining setting.

With narrow curves and elevation changes, this technical circuit is a true challenge, featuring 23 demanding turns and an underground section that adds to the excitement.

It is a race that impresses with a relatively young history, but its popularity continues to grow.

Humidity and heat pose physical tests, while the artificial lighting makes it even more complex.

Yet, the thrill and speed are magical on this circuit that fascinates every year.

Which race are we referring to?

a) Abu Dhabi Grand Prix.
b) Bahrain Grand Prix.
c) Singapore Grand Prix.

52

My logo is a mythical, noble, and elegant animal that symbolizes power, grace, and constant movement.

My presence in Formula 1 is synonymous with prestige, and my sophisticated style is recognized worldwide.

Sponsoring renowned teams is my specialty, and my presence in Formula 1 is a testament to my quality.

On the race tracks, my image exudes elegance, and my Pegasus logo is an emblem of distinction and relevance.

My luxury vehicles are admired for their design, and my classic and timeless style is a testament to that.

My name is synonymous with elegance and sophistication, and my presence in Formula 1 is an example of my dedication.

Which brand are we referring to?

a) The Rolls-Royce brand.
b) The Bentley brand.
c) The Aston Martin brand.

53

In the circuits of the world, there is a pilot of ice and fire.

His name is a melody that drives motor fans crazy.

He achieved the title with Ferrari, but he has also excelled in other teams because his talent has always shone through.

With his cool and calculated style, he doesn't let emotions guide him.

Thus, every move of the steering wheel is precise, and victory is a highly feasible option.

He has stood on the podium many times with his unique and special style, which has made him beloved and respected by fans in every country and city.

Who is this incredibly fast pilot?

a) Lewis Hamilton.
b) Fernando Alonso.
c) Kimi Räikkönen.

54

In Italy, there is a place with a very special circuit where engines roar incessantly, and speed is paramount.

It is known for its long and fast straight where cars reach their peak, and drivers hold on to their lives while their hands sweat from an adrenaline rush.

Speed is the law, and fans gather in every corner to watch brave pilots race on a legendary track that will never die.

Since 1922, it has witnessed great feats and legends that have left their mark and made history, such as Fangio, Ascari, Clark, and Senna with their skills, or the more recent Hamilton, who has left his euphoria.

It is a magical and sacred place where racing enthusiasts are acclaimed by 118,000 spectators, and the fastest circuits are crowned with victory, trophy, and earned honor.

Which circuit are we referring to?

a) Hungaroring.
b) Circuit Gilles Villeneuve.
c) Monza Circuit.

55

In the world of Formula 1, speed is the key to success.

The meticulously designed single-seaters by teams of engineers become true racing machines that must withstand extreme temperatures and incredibly high speeds.

One of the components that suffers the most is the exhaust system, which is subjected to very demanding conditions.

In each race, the exhaust pipes of Formula 1 cars heat up to unimaginable levels.

This temperature is extremely high and reflects the amount of heat generated inside the combustion engine.

F1 teams constantly work on improving their exhaust systems to reduce temperature and increase engine efficiency.

Additionally, the materials used in the construction of the exhaust pipes are highly advanced and heat-resistant, allowing them to withstand extreme temperatures without damage.

Despite the extreme temperatures they are subjected to, these components continue to function perfectly and enable F1 cars to reach impressive speeds.

What temperature do the exhaust pipes reach?

a) 800 degrees Celsius.
b) 1000 degrees Celsius.
c) 1200 degrees Celsius.

56

What speed do the cars reach at the start of the race?

It is an astonishing figure that is hard to surpass, as Formula 1 cars can accelerate as fast as a hurricane.

Keep in mind that this time can vary, as it depends on the type of tire they have on the track or the traction they can generate.

How many seconds do they need to go from 0 to 100 km/h?

a) 2.6 seconds.
b) 3.0 seconds.
c) 2.8 seconds.

57

Since my childhood, I dreamed of speed.

The passion for racing led me to a great place, hand in hand with my talent and dedication.

Nowadays, my career is a great sensation.

I was born in lands of wine and cheese, a place full of history and passion where I forged my great reason.

Since I was a child, my destiny was traced, to be a great driver was my golden desire.

With effort and perseverance, I reached the pinnacle where only the best reach.

My skill is unique, my ability unparalleled, as each race is a challenge, each victory unforgettable.

In 2017, I joined the Force India team, currently known as Aston Martin.

I achieved my first podium in Formula 1 at the 2020 Sakhir Grand Prix, finishing in second place.

I won my first race at the 2021 Hungarian Grand Prix.

I am a warrior on wheels, a hero on the track. With my eyes on the finish line, victory is within sight.

My team is my squad, family, and home, for together we are invincible and together we will triumph.

Who am I?

a) Esteban Ocon.
b) Nicholas Latifi.
c) Yuki Tsunoda.

58

In the world of racing, the shine and adrenaline are lived with passion in every turn and straight, and even more so when a rookie dares to fight for the top to make their name resound loudly.

It is well known that debuting in Formula 1 is a dream that few achieve, and whoever does it successfully will undoubtedly be remembered forever as a great champion.

That is why there is a very special award that is given to the most outstanding debutant.

It is a valuable object, a symbol of excellence that fills every rookie with pride and satisfaction.

Its shape is majestic, with fine and precise details, a bronze plate that shines with its own light, a trophy that is not only for the winner but for the one who achieves a great feat in their debut.

What award are we referring to?

a) The Rookie of the Year Award.
b) The Distinction for the Best Debut of the Season.
c) The Rookie of the Year Plaque.

59

In a place in the Mediterranean where the roar of engines resonates, the drivers compete with great passion to claim victory in their eagerness.

This circuit is a constant challenge with curves that defy skill and straights that invite speed, where the wind blows strongly and resolutely.

Every year in spring, this great celebration takes place, where the best drivers fight with all their determination and skill.

The Grand Prix of this land is a world-class event that attracts motor sports fans and makes the crowd vibrate.

The Montmeló circuit is the perfect stage for cars to run freely and drivers to showcase their talent.

Which Grand Prix are we referring to?

a) The Italian Grand Prix at the Monza Circuit.
b) The Spanish Grand Prix at the Circuit de Barcelona-Catalunya.
c) The French Grand Prix at the Paul Ricard Circuit.

60

If thirst assails you and you want to refresh yourself, my brand, you must seek and drink without fear.

In Formula 1, I sponsor with great enthusiasm, and my logo with 3 stars is a great emblem of taste and glamour.

My cocktails are famous, my blends very refined.

With gin or vermouth, you can prepare whatever you prefer.

My history is rich, born in Italy, and can be enjoyed worldwide.

I am the preferred liquor of secret agents.

Who am I?

a) Campari.
b) Aperol.
c) Martini.

61

I am a riddle about a driver who showcased his great talent on the tracks.

Of Australian origin, rising in fame, he left his legacy printed in Formula 1.

He won races, poles, and podiums without ceasing, and in his career as a driver, he always stood out unmatched.

With a smile on his face and a special charisma, he conquered his fans, who will always be by his side.

Years went by, and his career came to an end, but his legacy on the track remained engraved.

His name was written in the history of F1, and in the memory of fans, it will always be kept.

His career was long and filled with successes; he had great moments at Red Bull.

He always competed on an equal footing with Weber, and their on-track duel was always sensational.

Who was this star driver?

a) Mark Webber.
b) Jenson Button.
c) Felipe Massa.

62

I am located in Italian lands.

My layout is fast, and relentless curves make me a challenge for highly talented drivers.

My name comes from the land, a valley of unparalleled beauty, with landscapes that leave a mark and a history that is ancestral.

I was recently inaugurated in the world of Formula 1, to the delight of everyone.

Inside me, up to 84,000 fans can fit; my fast curves are a delight for those seeking excitement, and each straight is a test of skill and precision.

I am a renowned circuit that has made many sigh.

Do you already know my name and in which country you can find me?

a) Mugello Circuit in Italy.
b) Estoril Circuit in Portugal.
c) Spielberg Circuit in Austria.

63

In the world of Formula 1, the most powerful teams are those of the elite, such as Mercedes, Ferrari, McLaren, and Red Bull, where hundreds of people work tirelessly without rest.

To ensure the success of the cars on the track, engineers, mechanics, and designers are needed, who take care of every detail with care and dedication, always ready for competition.

Many people work in these high-performance teams so that the 2 cars can achieve glory with their speed, power, and precision.

But other teams have less budget and cannot afford as many employees, so they must be more clever and creative to compete against the big competitors.

How many people approximately work in a team?

a) 600 people.
b) 400 people.
c) 200 people.

64

In Formula 1, speed is crucial, and gear changes are essential to reach maximum speed on the track.

Throughout the laps covered during a race, many speed changes are made.

The exact number depends on the length and complexity of the circuit, as well as the duration of the race.

In shorter and more complex circuits, drivers have to make more gear changes, while in longer circuits with fewer corners, the number of changes is lower.

However, it should be noted that the number of gear changes also depends on the type of gearbox used in the car.

Currently, most teams use an 8-speed gearbox, which allows greater control over the car's speed on the track.

What is the approximate number of gear changes a driver makes in a race?

a) 2,000–3,000 gear changes.
b) 2,500–4,000 gear changes.
c) 4,000–5,000 gear changes.

65

In the world of Formula 1, there is a fierce rivalry between two highly talented drivers, both with great skill.

On one hand, we have a Spanish driver who conquers, and on the other hand, an Australian driver who is always ready to deliver.

The first one, known as "El Matador," has the fire of passion and love for motorsport in his blood.

With his experience and cunning, he knows well how to maneuver, and with a smile on his face, he is always ready to fight.

On the other hand, the Australian driver is fearless and always willing to attack with exceptional skill.

With his driving style and knack for spectacle, he is one of the most beloved drivers by the passionate audience.

Although both are highly talented, there is an underlying rivalry that has emerged in some races and has become very heated.

However, despite the tensions, there is respect between the two because they know that in the end, in Formula 1, there can only be one winner.

Which drivers are we referring to?

a) Antonio Giovinazzi and Lando Norris.
b) Sebastian Vettel and Sergio Perez.
c) Carlos Sainz and Daniel Ricciardo.

66

In the roar of engines, speed is king, and in every corner and straight, the challenge is constant.

But that driver who achieves the fastest lap receives an honor that turns them into a giant.

This trophy is an exclusive object worthy of admiration, specially designed for the occasion.

Its shape is a work of art, a jewel of competition that reflects the greatness of the driver and their passion.

It is a trophy awarded in every race, symbolizing the courage and dedication of the driver who dares to challenge speed and conquer the circuit with great skill.

Its details are refined and precise, and its value is incalculable for the recipient, as it represents the dedication and effort required to be the fastest on the circuit.

Which award am I referring to?

a) The Trophy for the Fastest Circuit.
b) The Distinction for the Driver with the Fastest Lap of the Season.
c) The Award for the Fastest Driver in a Single Lap.

67

In a land of snowy rivers and lakes, where there is a city overflowing with charm, engines purr with passion on a circuit that is pure fascination.

The roar of the cars can be heard from afar as the drivers take to the track, seeking glory and victory in an action-packed and adrenaline-filled Grand Prix.

The circuit is the stage for this great race, where cars race at high speeds, and the crowd cheers with joy.

On this special track, the drivers challenge their skills with tight corners and a long straight that invites the cars to go at full speed.

The Grand Prix of this land is a highly exciting competition that makes fans thrill and leaves the drivers with a pounding heart.

Which Grand Prix are we referring to?

a) The Australian Grand Prix.
b) The Singapore Grand Prix.
c) The Canadian Grand Prix.

68

In Formula 1 races, I am a well-known name for my great reliability and solidity that have distinguished me.

Like a great rock, my brand remains strong, sponsoring with determination and great commitment in every race that comes along.

My logo with a diamond shape is a symbol of stability and trust in my ability to reach any goal with safety.

On the race track, my team is always prepared to compete bravely and achieve success without ever being intimidated.

With their powerful engines and extensive experience, I have been a loyal sponsor in Formula 1 with great consistency.

With a constant commitment to innovation and technology, I continue to be a leader in the world of motorsport, there is no doubt about it.

Who am I?

a) Mercedes-Benz.
b) Renault.
c) Toyota.

69

I will give you certain clues and facts about a driver you know well.

He is British and a true master of the wheel.

World champion in 2009, he stood atop the podium.

He broke youth records when he made his debut, and many have followed in his footsteps.

With elegance and style, he races on the track, a natural talent that few ignore.

You will see him in a red and silver team, shining with the number eleven on his car.

A champion who put an end to races and to the world of triumphs.

Who is this driver?

a) Jenson Button.
b) Lewis Hamilton.
c) Sebastian Vettel.

70

From the curves and straights of my layout, the drivers navigate with care.

My name derives from my location.

I am a place where asphalt reigns supreme, and skill is required in my design, as tight corners are my specialty, where brakes and traction are the key to victory.

My history is rich in emotions with triumphs by great champions like Senna, Schumacher, and Hamilton who have brought their prowess to victory.

Which circuit are we referring to?

a) Valencia Circuit.
b) Hungaroring Circuit.
c) Yas Marina Circuit.

71

Car racing has always been a passion for speed and adrenaline enthusiasts, and Formula 1 is the queen of them all.

It all began in Europe at a time when aviation was booming, and combat pilots were eager to showcase their skills.

Thus, car races began to take place on makeshift circuits at airfields, gradually becoming more professional.

In 1946, a group of European businessmen decided to create an internationally recognized category of motorsport, and that's how Formula 1 was born.

The first race was held in 1950 at Silverstone, England, and since then, it has become a global phenomenon.

How many people were involved in the creation of this category?

a) 5.
b) 10.
c) 20.

72

In the world of Formula 1, speed is the key to success, and the pit crew plays a crucial role in it.

In just a few seconds, they can change the tires and refuel the car, allowing the driver to get back on the track as quickly as possible.

Mechanics train for hours on end to achieve the fastest time, working in sync to ensure everything is swift and efficient.

But it's not all about skill; technology also plays an important role.

The compressed air guns used to loosen and tighten the tire screws have a capacity of up to 30,000 rpm, enabling them to perform their job in a matter of milliseconds.

It's important to mention that the speed of the pit stop can vary depending on the team and circumstances.

In some cases, it may take a little longer due to technical or mechanical issues with the car.

Approximately how long does a pit stop take to change tires and refuel the car?

a) 5 seconds.
b) 1 second.
c) 3 seconds.

73

Two rivals on the track face each other with skill and extreme speed.

They both compete with the aim of victory, and the rivalry between them is intense.

One, with an aggressive and dominant style, seeks to surpass their adversary relentlessly with bold and precise maneuvers, trying to leave the other behind without mercy.

On the other hand, the other, calmer and more calculated, measures each move with caution.

They are cunning and skillful in every turn and know when the opportune moment to attack is.

Both have a great trajectory in Formula 1, multiple victories and achievements distinguish them, but only one can take the glory and leave their rival behind in this endless race.

Which drivers are we referring to?

a) Carlos Sainz and Daniel Ricciardo.
b) Max Verstappen and Charles Leclerc.
c) Fernando Alonso and Jenson Button.

74

In the excitement of the race, when the pack is in turmoil and cars vie for each position, there is a moment of glory when a daring driver makes an overtaking move that garners admiration.

It is an instance of skill and dexterity that requires courage and strategy, and when successfully executed, it becomes a feat deserving recognition and celebration.

That is why this special trophy was created, to honor the driver who makes the best overtaking maneuver, an artwork symbolizing the greatness of the one who achieves the most spectacular move.

It is an exclusive piece, specially designed, and renewed each season to surprise.

Its value is incalculable, as it represents the ability and courage required to conquer.

Which award are we referring to?

a) The Trophy for the Best Overtaking Move of the Race.
b) The Distinction for the Driver with the Most Spectacular Maneuver.
c) The Award for the Driver Who Executes the Most Incredible Overtake.

75

In a vibrant and colorful city, the roar of engines is heard on a circuit that poses a challenge for passionate and skilled drivers.

The first Grand Prix of the year is held in this dreamlike city, on an urban circuit that tests the drivers' abilities.

The Albert Park Circuit is famous for its tight corners and directional changes that thrill the fans and test the cars' required precision.

The drivers hit the track with determination, seeking victory and glory in their race, facing a circuit that offers no respite in a fierce battle for victory.

This Grand Prix marks the beginning of a season full of excitement and passion, which will thrill fans and leave the drivers with their hearts pounding.

Which Grand Prix are we referring to?

a) Bahrain Grand Prix
b) Australian Grand Prix.
c) Singapore Grand Prix.

76

If innovation is what you're passionate about, then you should consider my brand.

In Formula 1, I sponsor with great creativity and technology, and my track record in the automotive world is impressive.

I am a company with over 200 years of history, founded in France in the 19th century.

Since then, we have been pioneers in the production of cutting tools, bicycles, engines, cars, and other vehicles.

Today, we are recognized for our commitment to quality, safety, and design.

In Formula 1, my team has achieved significant victories and made its mark in the competition.

Our cars are always at the forefront of technology, and our team of engineers and designers works tirelessly to improve their performance.

My logo is a brand emblem, a rampant feline symbolizing boldness, strength, and progress.

Since 1858, this image has been associated with quality, innovation, and creativity.

Which brand am I referring to?

a) Mercedes-Benz.
b) BMW.
c) Peugeot.

77

On the track, he is a swift lightning bolt.

His skill is evident in the corners, and his prowess in the rain is unmatched. His name in Formula 1 is a great honor.

Born in Latin America, he is a champion who fears no risk.

His talent on the track is a spectacle that fills everyone with admiration and joy.

He boasts victories and records, and speed is his greatest strength.

His driving style is a feat that keeps the audience and rivals in suspense.

He shone between McLaren and Williams, and although he no longer competes in Formula 1 today, his legend in the sport will always live on, for he is a great driver that history will not forget.

He won the 2001 Italian Grand Prix in his debut season with the Williams-BMW team, delivering a fantastic race by overtaking Michael Schumacher on the last lap to claim victory.

He also won the 2003 Monaco Grand Prix during his third season in Formula 1, again with the Williams-BMW team, prevailing after an intense battle with Kimi Räikkönen.

Who is this fearless driver whose talent on the track made us thrill?

a) Juan Pablo Montoya.
b) Sergio Pérez.
c) Rubens Barrichello.

78

In the land of tequila, you'll find this race track, a high-speed circuit that many want to win.

With its altitude, engines need more power and acceleration, and the track winds through the streets of the capital with tight curves and a long final straight.

With a length of 4.304 kilometers, drivers prepare for a battle of endurance and attitude.

Since 2015, it has been celebrated and has witnessed great moments that thrill the 110,000 spectators who fit in this place.

What is the name of this circuit?

Possible answers:

a) Autódromo Oscar y Juan Gálvez.
b) Circuito de Jerez.
c) Autódromo Hermanos Rodríguez.

79

In Formula 1, the weight of the cars is crucial.

Every gram counts, every detail is vital, but the main rule is clear: the minimum weight must be respected until the end.

The marked threshold is fundamental, undoubtedly a challenge for the engineers.

With composite carbon fiber as the material, the cars are very light, with great efficiency and quality.

Before 2014, cars used to add ballast to meet the requirement, a significant effort.

Nowadays, teams have an even greater challenge, to maintain the correct weight and make the car faster.

What is the minimum weight of a Formula 1 car without fuel?

a) 754 kg.
b) 798 kg.
c) 845 kg.

80

In the pinnacle of motorsport, the engine is one of the key components of the car.

It is responsible for converting the chemical energy of the fuel into mechanical energy to propel the vehicle.

However, in Formula 1, engines have a limited lifespan due to the high revolutions and demands they are subjected to, which means that each team must carefully manage the amount of power used in each race to avoid premature engine failure.

However, engine manufacturers continue to work on improving the durability of these engines, seeking ways to maximize power while extending their lifespan.

What is the average lifespan of an F1 engine?

a) 7 races.
b) 10 races.
c) 5 races.

81

On the tracks of the world, two rivals met.

Both with skills that impressed everyone.

One with a cool and calculated style, the other with unmatched aggression.

For many years, they had never competed head-to-head, but when they did, everyone was amazed.

In each race, an epic battle unfolded with thrilling overtakes that captivated everyone.

One of them is known by the nickname "Iceman," while the other is called "Mr. Consistency."

Both are world champions, both have great talent.

Which drivers are we referring to?

a) Valtteri Bottas and Daniel Ricciardo.
b) Kimi Räikkönen and Lewis Hamilton.
c) Fernando Alonso and Max Verstappen.

82

At the top of the mountain, where effort is rewarded and the journey traveled is crowned with glory, lies the most coveted trophy of all, one that only the best in Formula 1 have obtained.

This object is a symbol of triumph and perseverance, a treasure that can only be won with skill and expertise.

It is an award presented in a majestic ceremony that pays tribute to the best of the year.

It is the most important of all, a unique and exclusive piece that represents the greatness of the one who has surpassed their rivals and emerged as the best in the competition.

This object, designed with artistry and elegance, is the culmination of a season of hard work, a treasure that will be remembered forever by the one who has proven to be the best of all.

Which award are we referring to?

a) The Decade's Best Driver Statue.
b) The Championship Trophy.
c) The Fastest Driver Award.

83

In a land of opportunities and dreams, engines roar with strength and passion on a circuit that is a true challenge for ambitious drivers.

It is celebrated on an impressive circuit surrounded by mountains and nature that makes hearts beat faster.

The circuit features tight turns and elevation changes that test the skill of the drivers and challenge the precision of the cars.

The drivers battle for victory in an exciting Grand Prix that thrills fans and leaves the racers breathless.

This Grand Prix is important for Formula 1 and especially for chili lovers, as it is a grand celebration where racing enthusiasts and the occasional cowboy gather to enjoy a world-class competition.

Which Grand Prix are we referring to?

a) The Mexican Grand Prix at the Hermanos Rodríguez circuit.
b) The Brazilian Grand Prix at the Interlagos circuit.
c) The United States Grand Prix at the Circuit of the Americas.

84

If time is what you're passionate about, then you should consider my brand.

In Formula 1, I sponsor with great precision and accuracy.

My logo, with a shield, is a symbol of tradition and excellence.

I am a watch brand with a long history and a great global reputation.

My timepieces are known for their quality and elegance and have become a symbol of status and luxury.

My products have been used in exploring the most remote places on Earth, from the depths of the ocean to the highest peaks in the world.

My technological innovations have been recognized by the industry, and I have been awarded numerous prizes and distinctions.

My commitment to quality and excellence has been constant over the years, and my presence in Formula 1 is yet another testament to my dedication to precision and speed, as I have been used by some of the greatest drivers in history.

Which watch brand am I referring to?

a) Omega.
b) Rolex.
c) Cartier.

85

With a colorful helmet and a fast car, this British driver
is renowned.

His aggressive style made him famous, and he was always
courageous on the track.

With his mustache and determination, he won a significant
number of races, and in 1992, he claimed the championship,
an achievement that will never be forgotten.

Among the victories he obtained are:

- European Grand Prix: 1985, 1991.

- South African Grand Prix: 1992.

- Australian Grand Prix: 1985, 1986, 1994.

But it wasn't all smooth sailing for this driver, as a serious
accident left him battered, but his courage and perseverance
led him to regain his bravery and confidence.

In Formula 1, he made a name for himself known for his bravery,
earning tremendous fame.

Which driver are we referring to?

a) Nigel Mansell.
b) Eddie Irvine.
c) Damon Hill.

86

In the French lands, there is a circuit named in honor of a businessman known for his love of endless racing.

Its design is quite distinctive with blue, red, and black lines. It's a thrill for the drivers but beautiful to watch, with an endless straight that makes hearts tremble.

The greatest of all time have been seen here, from the legendary Ayrton Senna to Lewis Hamilton.

With challenging curves and exciting elevation changes, it poses a challenge for any driver without exception.

Amidst olive trees and the Provencal sun, the cars roar on the track, and the crowd passionately cheers as the drivers fight for the first place.

Which circuit are we referring to?

a) Red Bull Ring Circuit.
b) Paul Ricard Circuit.
c) Spa-Francorchamps Circuit.

87

My dear friend, let me tell you about a true engineering feat where precision and skill are employed.

In the pinnacle of motorsport, each Formula 1 car is assembled with numerous precise components that fit perfectly and leave no room for error to achieve the speed and performance of a great engine.

From the tires to the electronic systems, every detail is crucial in Formula 1 cars, as a small mistake anywhere could spell disaster in the upcoming race.

Aerodynamics, chassis, transmission are just some of the parts in this intricate construction, as each one must be designed and manufactured with great precision so that when assembled, they create a machine filled with great passion.

How many components does each car have?

a) 60,000 components.
b) 80,000 components.
c) 100,000 components.

88

The alarm sounds, the moment has arrived, the race begins, everything is set.

The cars roar, the crowds cheer, and on the track, the drivers prepare.

Brake discs are crucial at the start, and at high speeds, they are a vital tool, but the stress they endure is immense, and the heat they generate is a constant threat.

They can reach extreme temperatures and jeopardize the team's success, which must work with precision and speed to change the discs efficiently and skillfully.

What temperature can the brake discs reach?

a) 800 degrees Celsius.
b) 1200 degrees Celsius.
c) 1000 degrees Celsius.

89

At the circuit, a fiery rivalry formed.

Two exceptional drivers, both wanting to triumph at the highest level, intertwined their destinies in a clash of personalities driven by their passion and ambition, in a competition full of hostilities.

One with their bold and risky style pushes the limits, fearlessly embracing danger, seeking the thrill of victory and glory, hence their name is etched in golden letters.

The other has a more disciplined and methodical approach, driving with precision, strategy, and technique, perfecting every detail of their craft in pursuit of victory in each race.

Their lives intersected in a battle for supremacy.

On the circuit, tension was palpable with every overtake and maneuver.

On the track, neither was willing to yield, driving to the limit, unafraid of death or fading away.

The rivalry reached its climax in an epic season.

There was a shocking accident in which one of them nearly lost their life, but their competitive spirit never waned, and even after it all, their rivalry endured.

Which drivers are we referring to?

a) Ayrton Senna and Alain Prost.
b) Lewis Hamilton and Nico Rosberg.
c) Sebastian Vettel and Mark Webber.

90

In the desert of black gold, a luxurious Grand Prix is celebrated, where cars race relentlessly on a captivating circuit.

The sun slowly sets on the horizon, and the city lights illuminate, while the engines roar loudly on a circuit that surprises everyone.

Cars race in an exhilarating competition, where speed combines with the beauty of the surroundings in harmony.

The circuit is a masterpiece with an innovative and unique design, featuring tight corners and long straights that make the race thrilling and epic.

The Grand Prix is an event that attracts speed enthusiasts, in a place where wealth is evident, and the spectacle is unparalleled.

Which Grand Prix are we referring to?

a) The Bahrain Grand Prix.
b) The Abu Dhabi Grand Prix.
c) The Malaysian Grand Prix.

91

In Formula 1, speed is crucial, and my brand knows it well.

We sponsor with great precision and accuracy because we know that every second counts in this competition.

We are a globally renowned brand, recognized for our quality.

Our logo features the colors green, white, and red, symbolizing our long tradition in manufacturing high-end watches.

These have been used by some of the greatest F1 drivers in history, including Ayrton Senna, Alain Prost, and Lewis Hamilton.

We pride ourselves on constant innovation and the pursuit of excellence.

We are the result of years of experience and refinement, known for our durability and reliability in extreme conditions.

Dedication to precision, quality, and craftsmanship is our guarantee, and we are proud to be an integral part of the competition.

Which brand are we referring to?

a) Tag Heuer.
b) Omega.
c) Breitling.

92

With four championship titles to his name, his style is smooth and cunning as he races.

This skillful French driver won epic battles on the unmatched track.

In his youth, he was considered a rookie, but soon proved to be a natural-born racing driver, flawlessly maneuvering his car with mastery, leaving his rivals behind with great skill and bravery.

His rivalry with Senna was legendary and well-known, their duels on the track were an unmatched spectacle, and although his driving style was more calculated, he would stop at nothing to achieve victory with honor.

Hardworking and disciplined, always seeking improvement, he gave his all in every race without fear of taking risks, and although his career was successful and filled with unparalleled achievements, he never lost humility and passion for this unmatched sport.

Who is this driver of great legacy and honor?

a) Michael Schumacher.
b) Alain Prost.
c) Ayrton Senna.

93

In a dreamlike country in the middle of the sea, a racing circuit was built in its place.

With long straights and tight curves, the drivers maneuver daringly on it.

The hot sun makes the drivers sweat as they give their best with their engines in every race.

With a track that changes depending on the day, strategy is key to achieving victory.

This track is located on a luxurious island, which has seen champions race with great vision, as from Hamilton to Vettel, they have fought in it with great fervor, shine, and stratagem.

Which circuit are we referring to?

a) Yas Marina Circuit.
b) Sakhir Circuit.
c) Sepang Circuit.

94

In past times, on the racing tracks, an experienced man won without barriers.

His age was not an impediment, his name is remembered, as today's youth hardly surpasses him.

An exceptional driver with strength and skill proved that age is not the only certainty.

He was a bold Italian, and in the French Grand Prix, his legend began to shine.

With 53 years to his account, victory came aboard his machine, as speed dominated.

Young rivals were surprised because, thanks to his experience and wisdom, he emerged victorious.

Which driver are we referring to?

a) Alberto Ascari.
b) Giuseppe Farina.
c) Luigi Fagioli.

95

A swift lightning on the burning asphalt, a daring driver achieved his record.

An unparalleled speedster roared on the track, writing his feat at an impressive velocity.

In Baku in the year 2016, a Finnish driver established a record.

With a high-tech Formula 1, he reached a speed of 378 km/h.

Many other drivers attempted to surpass that seemingly difficult mark.

One was a skilled German, another an energetic and vibrant Spaniard, and the third a Brazilian seeking final glory, but none succeeded.

The history of Formula 1 will remember his feat, and his speed will be hard to surpass.

This audacious driver demonstrated his skill and courage, leaving a message on the track.

The speed record will be difficult to match, and his feat will always remain in memory.

Which driver are we referring to?

a) Sebastian Vettel.
b) Kimi Räikkönen.
c) Valtteri Bottas.

96

On the Formula 1 tracks, a rivalry emerged with great passion between two exceptional drivers with unique personalities.

One has a more carefree style, while the other is more serious and focused.

However, both seek victory in every race and in every story.

A tragic accident marked their destinies, and although their differences became evident, they never lost mutual respect in a world where competition is their attribute.

The season came to an end with one champion, and the other remained behind without complaining, but their rivalry will always be remembered as one of the most exciting in this sport.

Which drivers are we referring to?

a) James Hunt and Niki Lauda.
b) Lewis Hamilton and Nico Rosberg.
c) Sebastian Vettel and Mark Webber.

97

In the heart of the Persian Gulf, in a kingdom of sun and sand, a Grand Prix is celebrated with rhythm on a circuit that dazzles everyone.

The desert envelops the atmosphere, the sun burns the skin, and the cars constantly accelerate on a circuit that defies the law.

The circuit is a place where speed is a religion, with tight corners and long straights where drivers demonstrate their passion.

The cars race at full speed on a circuit that tests their skill, where excitement knows no bounds.

The Grand Prix is an event that attracts speed enthusiasts in a place where luxury is evident, and the passion for Formula 1 is intense.

Which Grand Prix are we referring to?

a) The United Arab Emirates Grand Prix at the Yas Marina Circuit.
b) The Singapore Grand Prix at the Marina Bay Circuit.
c) The Bahrain Grand Prix at the Sakhir Circuit.

98

If elegance and design are what you're passionate about, then you must consider me.

I am a brand that sponsors F1 with great style and sophistication, and my logo features a majestic deer that is a symbol of elegance and distinction.

My watches are true works of art, created with high-quality materials and unmatched design.

I am a brand with a rich history founded over a century ago, always at the forefront of innovation and technology.

My products are highly appreciated for their elegance and exclusivity, used by people around the world who appreciate the utmost quality and design.

If you want to have a watch that reflects your good taste and love for design, then you must rely on me.

Who am I?

a) Jaeger-LeCoultre.
b) Girard-Perregaux.
c) Patek Philippe.

99

On the Formula 1 tracks, there is a female driver who is exceptional.

With her talent and passion, she has won many hearts.

She is a woman of great worth, who has conquered victory with her skill and prowess.

On board her race car, she showcases her great talent, and with her strength and courage, she has overcome many obstacles.

On a sad day for her, an accident left her injured, but her fighting spirit helped her move forward in life.

Today, she is an example for all women around the world, and her legacy in Formula 1 will always be remembered.

Who is this driver referring to?

a) María de Villota.
b) Ada Lovelace.
c) Malala Yousafzai.

100

By night, the lights come alive on this race track, as the speed machines navigate through it.

In the city of coconut milk, an impressive circuit is found.

Its crazy curves and straights surprise and captivate any driver.

The cars shine brightly like stars that are about to collide because every corner presents an interesting challenge for those who seek triumph.

In this place, a party is celebrated with glamour, luxury, and speed.

The spectacle is a thrill for any fan of adrenaline and competition.

What is the name of this circuit?

a) Circuit de Barcelona-Catalunya.
b) Autódromo José Carlos Pace.
c) Marina Bay Street Circuit.

101

Amidst the roar of engines and the bellow of the bull, my brand makes its presence known in F1, sponsoring with great passion and sportsmanship.

I am like a furious beast on the track, always seeking to surpass my competitors with the speed and strength that characterize me.

My logo with a horn is a great symbol of my power and energy, always ready to charge any obstacle in my way.

My designs are unique, encompassing style, sophistication, and sportiness.

If you seek excellence in every detail, you must consider my brand.

My presence in F1 has been a resounding success, achieving impressive results and standing out for my outstanding performance on the track.

Which brand are we referring to?

a) Aston Martin.
b) Ferrari.
c) Lamborghini.

Answers: 1-33.

1. c– Michael Schumacher.
2. c– Spa-Francorchamps.
3. a– Ferrari.
4. c– Nelson Piquet.
5. b– Lewis Hamilton and Fernando Alonso.
6. a– Formula 1 Constructors' Championship.
7. c– Ayrton Senna.
8. b– Versace.
9. c– Lewis Hamilton.
10. b– Silverstone Circuit.
11. a– Mercedes-AMG Petronas.
12. c– Lewis Hamilton.
13. b– Ayrton Senna and Alain Prost.
14. c– Sebastian Vettel.
15. a– Formula 1 World Championship Trophy.
16. a– Italian Grand Prix at Monza.
17. c– Mitsubishi.
18. c– Sebastian Vettel.
19. c– Monaco Circuit.
20. c– McLaren.
21. c– Fernando Alonso.
22. a– Nelson Piquet.
23. c– David Coulthard and Mark Webber.
24. a– Cap of the youngest driver to set a fastest lap in qualifying.
25. c– Belgian Grand Prix.
26. b– Pirelli.
27. b– Emerson Fittipaldi.
28. c– Suzuka Circuit.
29. c– Red Bull Racing.
30. a– Riccardo Patrese.
31. c– Rubens Barrichello.
32. a– Lewis Hamilton and Valtteri Bottas.
33. b– DHL Fastest Lap Award plaque.

34. c– Japanese Grand Prix.
35. b– Castrol.
36. c– Fernando Alonso.
37. a– Interlagos.
38. b– Alpine F1 Team.
39. c– Alain Prost.
40. a– Michael Schumacher and Rubens Barrichello.
41. a– Sebastian Vettel and Fernando Alonso.
42. b– Belgian Grand Prix Trophy.
43. b– Brazilian Grand Prix.
44. c– Shell.
45. c– Max Verstappen.
46. a– Spa-Francorchamps.
47. a– Up to 4 kg in weight.
48. a– Moisés Solana and Divina Galica.
49. c– Nico Rosberg and Jenson Button.
50. a– Trophy for the Driver with the Most Completed Laps.
51. c– Singapore Grand Prix.
52. c– Aston Martin brand.
53. c– Kimi Räikkönen.
54. c– Monza Circuit.
55. b– 1000 degrees Celsius.
56. a– 2.6 seconds.
57. a– Esteban Ocon.
58. c– Rookie of the Year Award.
59. b– Spanish Grand Prix at the Circuit de Barcelona-Catalunya.
60. c– Martini brand.
61. a– Mark Webber.
62. a– Mugello Circuit in Italy.
63. a– 600 people.
64. b– 2,500-4,000 gearshifts.
65. c– Carlos Sainz and Daniel Ricciardo.
66. b– Driver with the Fastest Lap of the Season distinction.
67. c– Canadian Grand Prix.

Answers: 68-101.

68. b- Renault.
69. a- Jenson Button.
70. b- Hungaroring Circuit.
71. b- 10 entrepreneurs, engineers, and motorsport enthusiasts were the creators of Formula 1.
72. c- 3 seconds.
73. a- Carlos Sainz and Daniel Ricciardo.
74. a- Trophy for the best overtaking maneuver of the race.
75. b- Australian Grand Prix at Albert Park Circuit in Melbourne.
76. c- Peugeot.
77. a- Juan Pablo Montoya.
78. c- Autódromo Hermanos Rodríguez.
79. b- 798 kg.
80. c- 5 races.
81. b- Kimi Räikkönen and Lewis Hamilton.
82. b- Championship Trophy.
83. c- United States Grand Prix at Circuit of the Americas in Austin, Texas.
84. b- Rolex.
85. a- Nigel Mansell.
86. b- Paul Ricard Circuit.
87. b- 80,000 components.
88. c- 1000 degrees Celsius.
89. a- Ayrton Senna and Alain Prost.
90. b- Abu Dhabi Grand Prix at Yas Marina Circuit.
91. a- Tag Heuer.
92. b- Alain Prost.
93. a- Yas Marina Circuit.
94. c- Luigi Fagiolini.
95. c- Valtteri Bottas.
96. a- James Hunt and Niki Lauda.
97. c- Bahrain Grand Prix at Sakhir Circuit.
98. c- Patek Philippe.
99. a- María de Villota.
100. c- Marina Bay Street Circuit.
101. c- Lamborghini.

If you have enjoyed the poetic riddles of Formula 1 presented in this book, we would like to ask you to share a review on Amazon.

Your opinion is extremely valuable to us and to other Formula 1 enthusiasts who are looking to be entertained and test their knowledge of this sport.

We understand that leaving a comment can be a tedious process, but we kindly ask you to take a few minutes of your time to share your thoughts and opinions with us.

Your support is very important to us and it helps us continue creating quality content for Formula 1 lovers.

Thank you for your support.

May your team always emerge victorious!

★ ★ ★ ★ ★

Printed in Great Britain
by Amazon

33791266R00066